Wonder & Delight
A Dolph Gotelli Christmas
Copyright © 2013 | Dolph Gotelli
Dolph Gotelli, author
www.dolphgotelli.net

Published in 2013 by
Half Full Press
1814 Franklin Street | Suite 603
Oakland, CA 94612
888.612-9908

ISBN- 13: 978-0-9855036-3-5

Printed and bound in China

right page: Haggin Museum | *Stockton, California*

To Ben —
With fond memories.
of our life long friendship
all christmas joys

With love
Dolph Sotelli
2016

Wonder & Delight

A DOLPH GOTELLI CHRISTMAS

4

As glad as Childhoods wakening smile may Christmas be to thee.

17

The Bountiful Bough

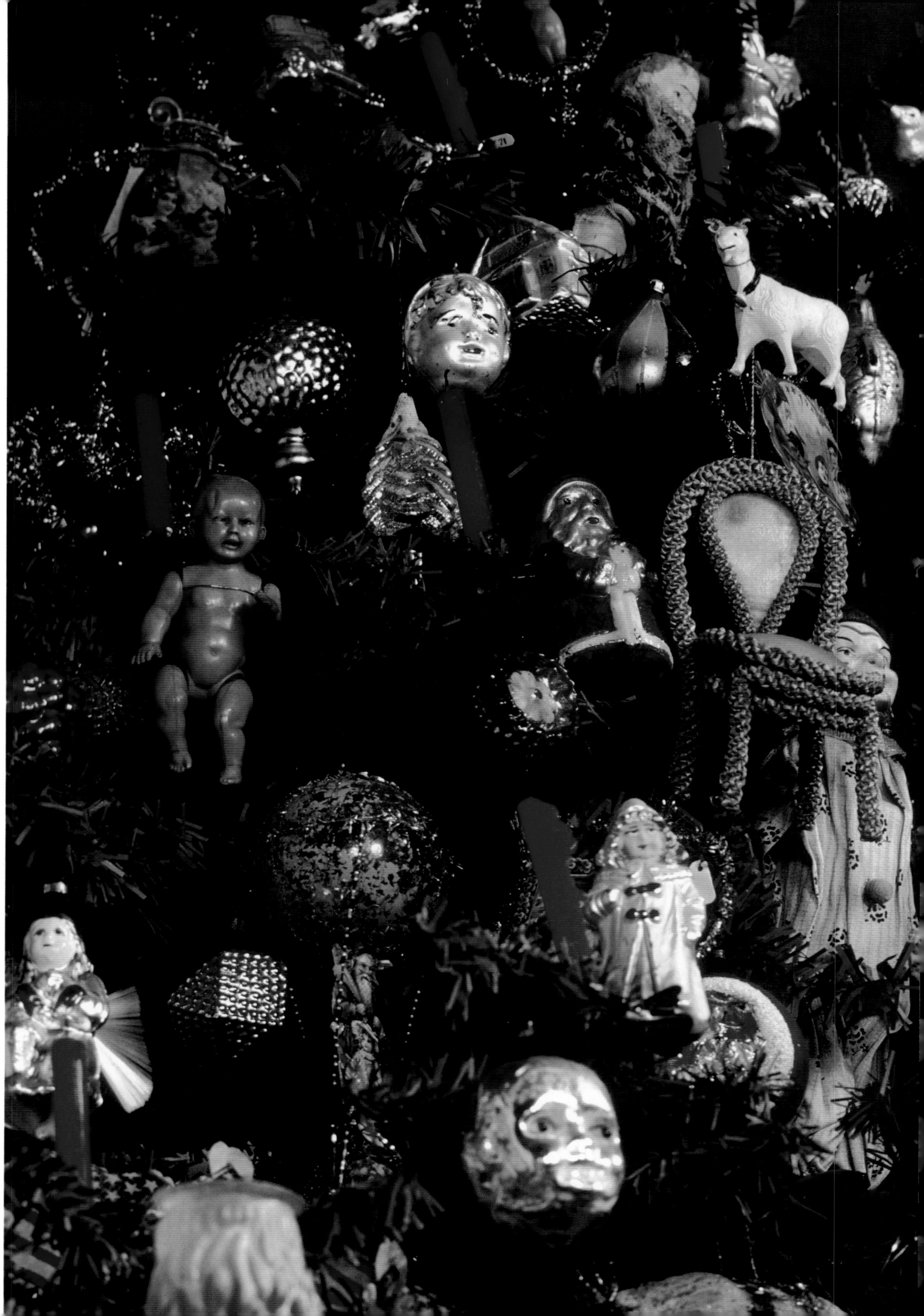

36

48

A VICTORIAN FANTASY TREE, DEDICATED TO THE CHILDLIKE WONDER OF CHRISTMAS

AUTHENTIC CHRISTMAS ANTIQUES
1860-1919
FROM THE COLLECTION OF DOLPH GOTELLI

Macy's | *San Francisco, California*

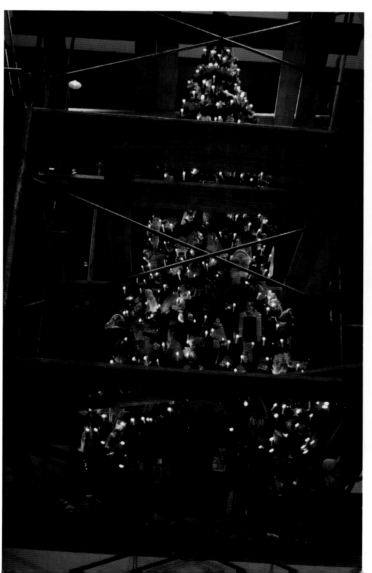

House or Museum?

The December 1981 issue of *Smithsonian* Magazine featured an article on my Christmas house, dedicating twelve pages to "A collector decks his halls with yuletide trove."

As a professor of design at the University of California, Davis, I formulated a two-pronged emphasis of study in exhibition design and visual presentation. At that time, the field of visual merchandising was thriving in retail. I invited my students seeking professional experience to work on my commercial ventures as a group study project. I had already accomplished a large exhibition on Santa Claus in a museum but finding venues for Christmas-themed exhibits was no easy task. My house, a late Victorian, lent itself as an interesting museum for an exhibition of Mexican folk art. I installed track lighting in my great room and made the most out of twelve-foot ceilings and several good-sized walls.

In 1980, I installed the first exhibition of Christmas decorations with a general theme. My team of interns removed furniture and stripped regular décor from the rooms. Since my entire collection was stored in my home, I would simply go to my storage area to retrieve a certain object, a far easier process than packing up and transporting objects to and from a museum.

House or Museum?

"My collecting interests presented another challenge for my decorating, that of combining diverse objects all working in the same environment ."

The second year's theme of a Victorian Christmas was more specific. The front parlor looked like a historic period room with borrowed Belter furniture, heavy window coverings and Santa emerging from the fireplace. As visitors entered the 22nd Street home, they would see a large tree looming ahead in the rotunda. The largest room had a gallery wall where I displayed my framed Christmas material. Antique frames of 19th-century die cuts, prints, and other ephemera covered the large wall of the great room.

Over a thousand viewers arrived for the Mother Goose tour—I always wondered what the neighbors thought when a busload of people would enter my home. The visitors were members of doll and toy clubs, service organizations, design staffs from department stores, and students from design schools.

"Mother Goose's Christmas Tour" was the most elaborate display, with every room put to good use. I even converted my studio, the one room I kept closed for storage, into a snowy forest with three papier-mâché trees serving as homes for dressed animals. Many articles in magazines and newspapers and television interviews documented these group tours in my home. Throughout the eighties, it certainly seemed I had my 15 minutes of fame.

My house was constantly evolving as an installation space. But after years of house tours and living with Christmas throughout my home—including my bedroom—until the take down in March, I decided to find other venues to present my work. The students never got involved with the take down, I needed to do this myself. With so much material, it had to be packed carefully and organized and stored by category.

Another challenge that I applied to my work was making diverse objects work together in a cohesive design. My other collections gained importance in my home and my interest in international masks and devotional art, including Latin American paintings, Santo figures and folk art, allowed me to do a different type of installation. My holiday decorating evolved into Victorian Christmas decorations, religious figures, Santa Claus and other objects all working in the same environment.

My house tours had one last revival in 2002. I was looking for a new home as my collections had outgrown the Victorian, so I decided to decorate one last time. A month later, I was still putting out much of my collection. Once I moved out of the house and into a rental, I realized that my home had truly become a museum. I had several fundraisers for the Design Museum at the University of California, Davis. As the founder and Director Emeritus of the museum, I was very happy with the response from the two years and at the end, 5,000 guests had come through the doors!

85

Dearest [...]
A cup of tea [...]
biscuit for you.
Happy Christmas
With love,
Clara

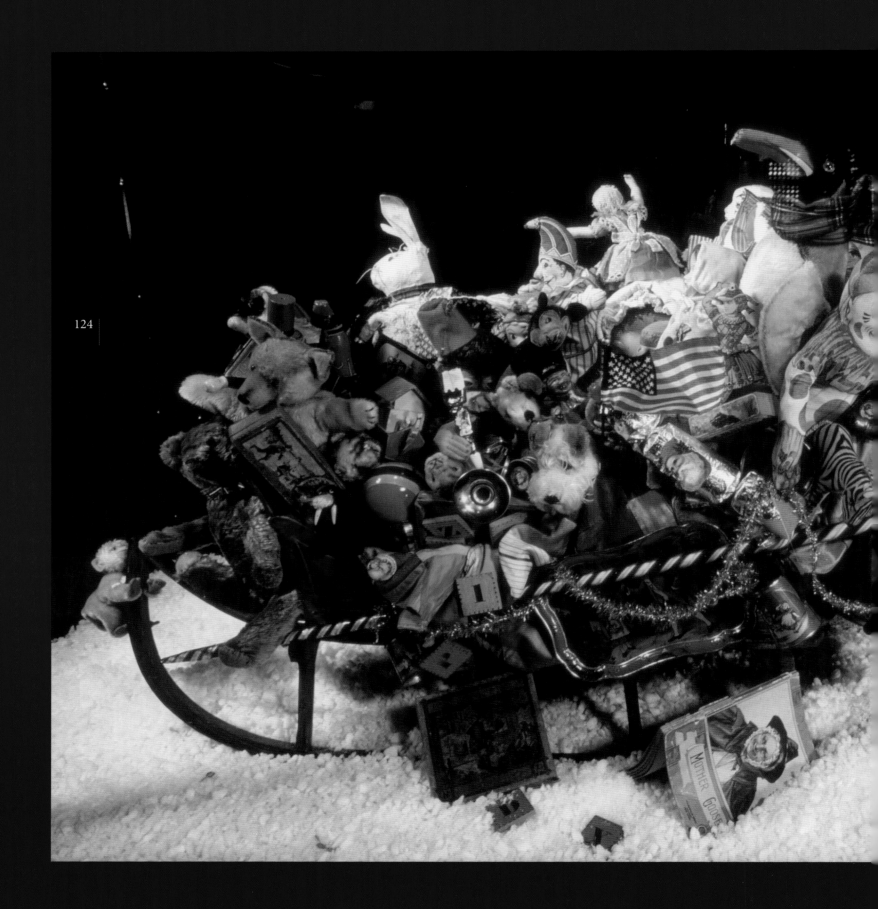

The Nut Tree | *Vacaville, California*

Neiman Marcus | *Dallas, Texas*

Nieman Marcus | *Dallas, Texas*

Trans America Pyramid, Lobby Gallery | *San Francisco, California*

"The Santa Show", Crocker Art Museum | *Sacramento, California*

The Art of Thomas Nast

"The Christmas Fantasies of Dolph Gotelli," Haggin Museum | *Stockton, California*

186

Filoli Mansion | *Woodside, California*

Napa Valley Museum | *Yountville, California*

264

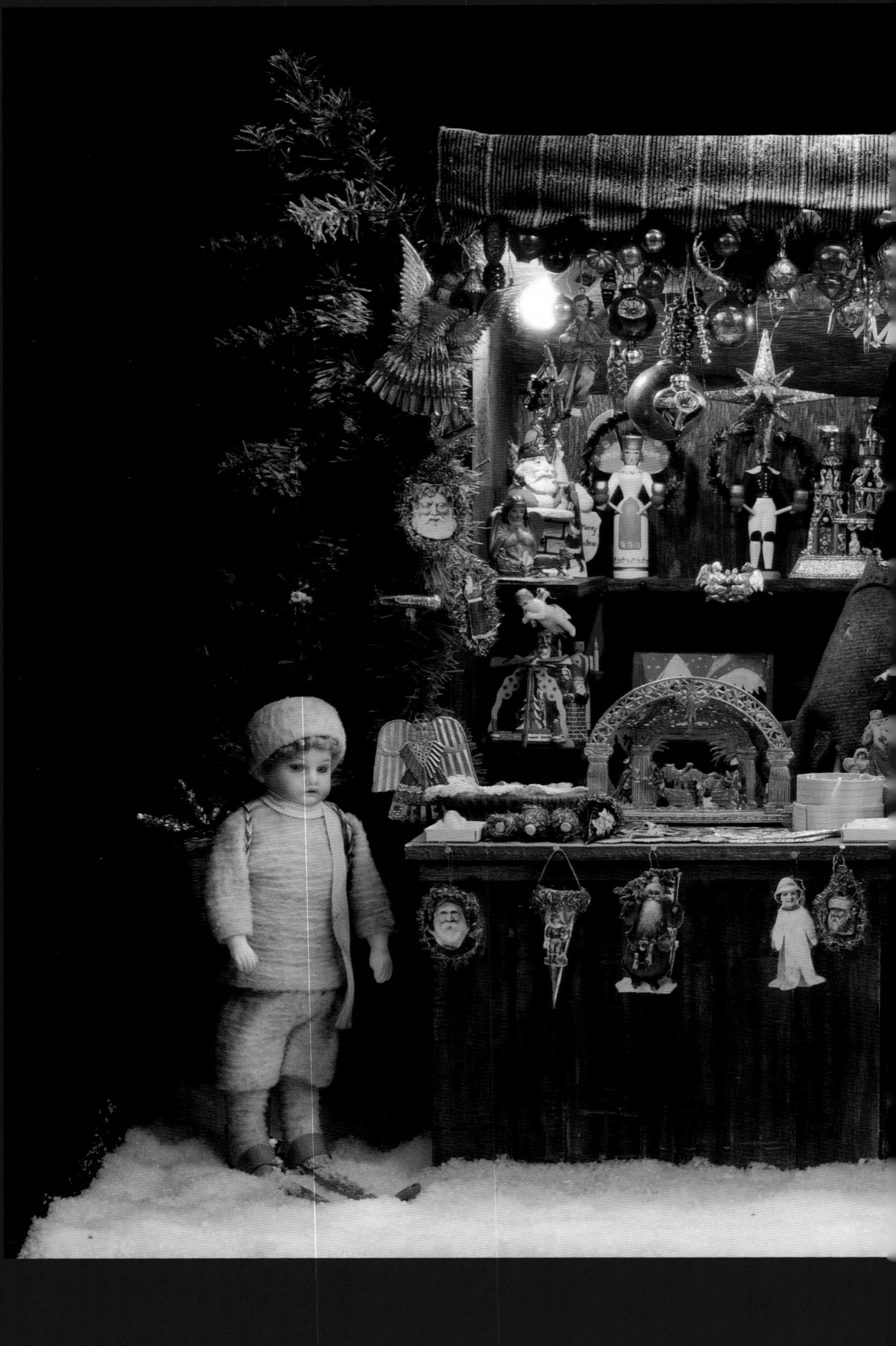

Fantasy Tablescapes

Since my first teaching position in the sixties, I have given all of my design classes the challenge of creating a "fantasy tablescape." I used this phrase because I wanted my students to get away from conventional table settings seen in magazines with coordinated dishes, glassware and floral centerpieces. I encouraged them to stretch their imaginations and generate original ideas to design a themed environment as the stage for presenting food and drink. They designed their own flatware out of vegetables and created drinking vessels and dishes out of unconventional materials. This concept has been carried forth in all my classes and workshops and is a format I like to repeat in my Christmas displays.

Fantasy Tablescapes

"A Christmas fantasy should be more than the eye can take in all at once."

I have gathered some examples from my past installations that show my Christmas versions of tablescapes, from toy sized to full scale. You may notice how much fun I have creating sugar plum party tables, utilizing my collections of chocolate Santa figures, colorful hard candies and frosted fruit along with antique Christmas china and other elements to push the fantasy as far as I can. Layers of sweets are arranged among candied trees, molded sugar figures, chocolate animals—all inhabitants of this edible tabletop.

It all relates to my interest in designing a dream environment of an edible landscape of sweets for the delight of children and adults alike.

When asked to decorate the formal dining room at the elegant Filoli mansion near San Francisco, I wanted to contrast the traditional room with a fantasy presentation. The tabletop was frosted entirely and the draped "tablecloth" flowing to the floor was made of simple white folded paper with doily accents.

I would have preferred to suspend the sugar-plum fairy from the overhead chandelier, but after a discussion with the house official, I ended up having her alight on the table.

The many tea party creations show my Baroque side: I think a Christmas fantasy should be more than the eye can take in all at once. It forces the over-stimulated spectators to choose individual elements on which to rest their eyes.

I have a growing collection of cakes, plum puddings, and delectable pastries made of wax, ceramic, plaster and assorted candies, both real and artificial, that I enjoy as my edible media. My goal is to blend these sweet ingredients into a Christmas fantasyland for all to savor.

A Passion for Paper

My attraction to paper occurred in the sixties when I first viewed a Victorian scrap of a Santa at a paper show.

After forty years of collecting ephemera, I realized that my taste was confined to Victorian and Edwardian periods. As a paper addict, I personally respond to the originality and whimsy of that unprecedented time. Strong colors and embossing techniques of chromolithography were at their peak during the 1880s.

Placement and display go hand in hand with my collections. Intuitively, I decided to hang paper on a tree as a good way to show off my ephemera without having to frame each piece. I added backing and hung them from loops, transforming my collection of Victorian curiosities into unique ornaments.

A Passion for Paper
"I am always attracted to something that I have not seen before and the world of Christmas paper is full of examples."

Upon discovering an old photo of a Christmas tree from 1901, I learned that my "invention," of hanging greeting cards, photos, die cuts and other ephemera on a Christmas tree was not unusual during that era, as documented in my collection of early photos of trees. At first, my eye was only on the St. Nicholas/Santa Claus imagery and I would not be happy with any other subject. But as I found so many brightly colored embossed die cuts with other subject matter, I enlarged my vision to include various images of 19th-century rituals, childhood characters and pure fantasy themes. The incessant variety of subject matter compelled me to keep searching for more. Rarely did I find the same designs in the search.

My attraction grew in depth and included any chromolithography die cut that caught my eye. Fantasy subjects included flower fairies, children in sugar bowls, Mother Goose nursery rhyme characters, anthropomorphic animals and, of course, St Nicholas in all his guises. When I started to decorate a Victorian tree for a museum, I added odd themes from the era and such non-Christmas images as crying babies, wild animals, cats and dogs, pretty children, fashionably dressed ladies and gentlemen, soldiers, interior household objects, famous monarchs and every imaginable insect. Christmas aside, my decorations have no boundaries. It is not unusual for me to hang a themed holiday paper piece on my tree. Valentines, Easter cards and Halloween decorations can be found among the branches.

I enjoy placing die-cut tinsel ornaments on garlands. I use "evergreen" garlands made of paper that do not harm the delicate ornaments. My collection of flat Dresdens (two-dimensional gold or silver embossed figures) display much better on garlands than on trees.

My addiction to ephemera had begun and no matter how many 12-step programs I begin, I am at the time of this writing still completely obsessed. I am always attracted to something that I have not seen before—and the world of Christmas paper is endless.

Graphic paper images never seem to escape my eye. When I attended my first East Coast Ephemera Society of America conference and show, a whole new world opened up. I found wonderful candy boxes with hanging strings, cornucopia with die-cut Santa heads, die-cut tinsel ornaments, little gift boxes, pressed cardboard animals and cotton-batting figures with scrap faces. To this array of whimsies, I purchased small three-dimensional greeting cards, die-cut trade cards and Victorian calendar prints that I also hung on my trees. Sunday school candy boxes, English Christmas crackers known as poppers, paper dolls and various paper toys always add an intriguing dimension to the festive tree.

I started mixing paper into my tree designs among conventional glass, toys and dolls that I attached to the limbs. This later evolved into one six-foot tree decorated entirely with paper. Soon after, I progressed to two six-foot trees with only paper material adorning its branches.

After many years of research, I discovered through my photo collections that during the early 19th century, paper ornaments were readily available for trimming. Die-cut chromolithographs of Santas, angels, children and other subject matter were readily available in stores. They were taken home

304

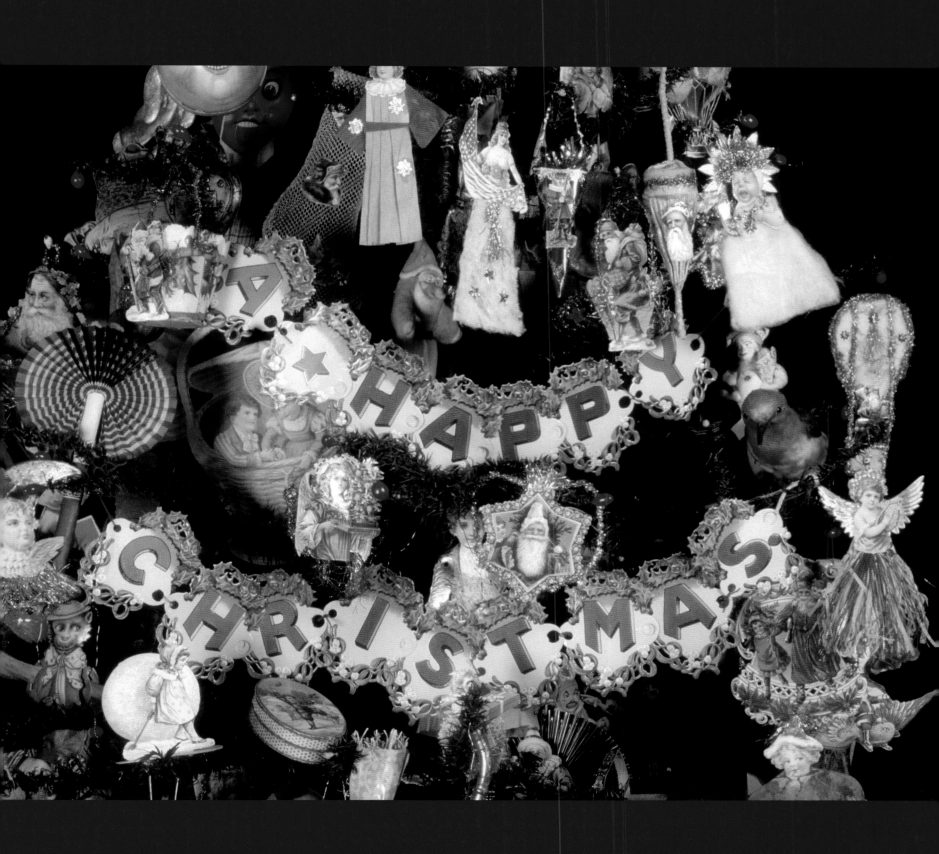

"Compliments of the Season: A Victorian Christmas," Crocker Art Museum | *Sacramento, California*

"Compliments of the Season: A Victorian Christmas," Crocker Art Museum | *Sacramento, California*

Decorating with Saints

325

325

336

343

349

Christmas Exhibitions by Dolph Gotelli

" A Child's Fantasy Tea Party," *An Elegant Celebration of Christmas, Design Center, San Francisco, California, 1978*

"The Santa Show," *Crocker Art Museum, Sacramento, California, 1977-78*

" The Enchantment of Christmas," *University Union Gallery, Sacramento State University, 1979*

"Fantasy Christmas House," *22nd St. Victorian, Sacramento, California, 1980*

"Christmas Past," *Macy's, Union Square, San Francisco, California, 1979-80*

"Animal's Christmas Fantasy," *The Nut Tree, Vacaville, California, 1979*

"Toy Tree," *An Elegant Celebration of Christmas, Design Center, San Francisco, California, 1979*

"Designer's Show House 1980," *Entry Hall, Sacramento, California, 1980*

"Fantasy of Christmas—Fountain Square," *Citrus Heights, California, 1980*

"The Magic of Santa Claus," *Chevron Gallery, San Francisco, California, 1981-82*

"Mother Goose's Christmas Tour," *22nd Street Victorian, Sacramento, California, 1982-83*

"Victorian Fantasy Tree," "St. Nicholas Shop of Wondrous Surprises," *Macy's, Union Square, San Francisco, California, 1983*

"A Victorian Christmas," *22nd Street Victorian, Sacramento, California, 1984*

"Christmas Fantasy," *Pumpkins and Monkeys, Pavilions Shopping Center, Sacramento, California, 1985*

" Christmas Fantasies of Dolph Gotelli," *Neiman Marcus Flagship Store, Dallas, Texas, 1986*

"Santa Claus is Coming to Town," *A Historical Look at the Merchandise, the Myth and the Meaning of Santa Claus, Civic Arts Center, Walnut Creek, California, 1988*

"The Christmas Fantasies of Dolph Gotelli," *Haggin Museum, Stockton, California, 1989-90*

"An Illustrated Christmas—19th Century Holiday Cards and Prints from the Collection of Dolph Gotelli," *Olive-Hyde Art Gallery, Fremont, California, 1990-91*

"Holiday Fantasies," *Transamerica Pyramid Gallery, San Francisco, California ,1991-92*

"Miracle on 46th Street," "A Spanish Colonial Christmas," *Designer's home tour, Sacramento, California, 1992*

"Objects of Christmas," Museum Room," *13th Annual Golden Glow of Christmas Past Convention, Palo Alto, California, 1993*

"A Gallery of Holiday Prints," *Alameda County Fairgrounds, Livermore, California, 1993*

357

"A World of Holiday Fantasies by Dolph Gotelli," *Lincoln Center, Stockton, California, 1993*

"Holiday Dreams," *Nimbus Winery, Rancho Cordova, California, 1995-96*

"The Celebration of Christmas—From the Collection of Dolph Gotelli," *McHenry Museum, Modesto, California, 1998*

"Holiday Fantasy," *Filoli Mansion, Woodside, California, 1999*

"A World of Toys: An International Exhibition," *Sacramento Central Library, Sacramento, California, 2000-01*

"Compliments of the Season: A Victorian Christmas by Dolph Gotelli," *Crocker Art Museum, Sacramento, California, 2001-02*

"An Enchanted Christmas by Dolph Gotelli," *Vacaville Museum, A Center for Solano County History, Vacaville, California, 2003-04*

"An Enchanted Christmas by Dolph Gotelli," *Folsom History Museum, Folsom, California, 2009-10*

"Dreams of Toyland," *Napa Valley Museum, Yountville, California, 2010-11*

"An Illustrated Christmas," *Folsom History Museum, Folsom, California, 2011-12*

"Dreams of Toyland," *Napa Valley Museum, Yountville, California, 2011-2012*

Acknowledgements

My appreciation must first be directed to my past students who worked with me on countless professional installations during my 35-year tenure at the University of California at Davis

So many of my Christmas displays could not have been completed without the support of scores of student interns, too numerous to name individually. I could never have succeeded without their creative assistance and skills. They drew, sewed, stapled, cut, frosted, glued, arranged, painted, cleaned, cataloged, built, carried, packed, unpacked, and so much more. Without their sincere dedication, I could not have achieved the voluminous amount of work presented in *Wonder & Delight*.

Special thanks to former students Robert Frye and Kim Fulton Hurst who, through the years, have devotedly assisted me with my Christmas installations, utilizing their special talents as professional colleagues and friends.

My thankfulness to the many individuals for their involvement with this book. My heartfelt gratitude to Gale Okumura and Caroline J. Thompson for their patience, technical and creative talents and steadfast commitment to me and my work.

Thank you to Christopher Radko for his kind remarks.

With fifty years of photographic documentation, the list of contributing photographers is vast, but my special thanks and admiration go to Barbara Molloy and C J. Thompson for their support and exceptional work.

My deepest gratitude to my numerous friends, family and anonymous visitors whom have faithfully followed my career and attended my exhibitions.

All Christmas joy be yours.